Rooms to Inspire
by the Sea

ANNIE KELLY
PHOTOGRAPHY BY TIM STREET-PORTER

RIZZOLI
NEW YORK

New York Paris London Milan

I must go down to the seas again, to the lonely sea and the sky,
And all I ask is a tall ship and a star to steer her by.
—*John Masefield, "Sea Fever"*

Acknowledgments

THIS BOOK WAS THE PERFECT SUMMER PROJECT, and we are grateful to everyone who opened their houses to us and included us in their lives while we were photographing them. We traveled north to Cape Cod to John Derian's captain's cabin and as far south as post-hurricane Harbour Island in the Bahamas. We would like to thank Tom Scheerer, David Flint Wood, and Olivier de Givenchy for all their help while we were on the island.

Thanks to Martyn Lawrence Bullard for flying us down to Mexico, and to Michael Green for the margaritas. Back in the U.S.A., Robert Couturier, Simon Doonan and Jonathan Adler, Matthew Patrick Smyth, Juan Montoya, and Florence de Dampierre on the East Coast and Peter Dunham in Los Angeles all gave us advice and encouragement. We are grateful to interior designer Tom Fallon for introducing us to Clora Kelly and Helge Skibeli on Shelter Island, and to Jack Deamer in Sag Harbor for helping us find storekeepers Chris Mead and Zoë Hoare (who also have incredible styling skills). Thanks to Susan White of *Vanity Fair*, and to decorator Julia Winston just for being her wonderful self.

Throughout the project Christin Markmann kept Tim's office working smoothly. Ashley Likins was a huge help with her retouching skills, while Mike Kelly was on standby for technical support.

We are very lucky to have a great Rizzoli book team: Sandy Gilbert, with her meticulous attention to detail, and the patience and skill of Doug Turshen. They were helped by Steve Turner, Marian Appelbaum, Jessica Napp, Hilary Ney, Elizabeth Smith, Jessica O'Neil, and publisher Charles Miers.

PAGE 1: *John Derian created a sitting room out of a landing in his Cape Cod house.*
PREVIOUS SPREAD: *The saltwater swimming pool and the Playhouse at Shangri La, 2011. Doris Duke Foundation for Islamic Art, Honolulu, Hawaii.* ABOVE: *Jenga the parrot sits on a watermelon at India Hicks and David Flint Wood's house on Harbour Island, Hibiscus Hill.* RIGHT: *Steven Gambrel framed fragments of a nautical-themed screen and hung them above his Sag Harbor fireplace.*

Contents

Introduction

THE SEA HAS ALWAYS FIGURED STRONGLY IN OUR IMAGINATION AND MYTHOLOGY. It represents many things for us—all life originally came from the ocean, and in Jungian psychology it is the symbol for the unconscious and deeper layers of the psyche. We are drawn to its sense of limitless space as a source of fresh air, along with the rhythmic sound of breaking waves and the cry of seagulls. The beach also symbolizes a more carefree and idealized way of life, stripped of the complications of the workaday world.

As soon as the weather becomes hot, we get an urge to leave life in the stifling cities behind and migrate to the water. Many of us have had our happiest childhood memories by the sea, although the life it represents appeals to both young and old. "I shall grow old . . . I shall wear white flannel trousers and walk along the beach," wrote the great Anglo-American poet T. S. Eliot. The theme of life at the beach is equally powerful in iconic movies like *Endless Summer*, a cheerful and optimistic 1966 surfing movie, and in moodier films like 1971's *Death in Venice*, where we get a sense that this is a slice of time set apart from normal life, where the customary rules no longer apply. Perhaps one of the strongest films to convey this is Fellini's 1965 *Juliet of the Spirits*, in which his wife, Giulietta Masina, played a discontented housewife installed in a perfect 1960s Italian house sitting almost directly on the sand.

Even though there are many different ways of living at the beach—whether in a Caribbean-style house on the water or an eighteenth-century ship captain's cottage, a rambling Shingle-style compound or

PREVIOUS SPREAD: *John Derian's house in Provincetown, Massachusetts, was once owned by a ship's captain.* ABOVE: *Decorator Tom Fallon spends most summers relaxing on his sun-dappled Shelter Island porch.* RIGHT: *A waterfront house with vibrant pink shutters on Harbour Island in the Bahamas.*

a mid-century modernist apartment building in Palm Beach, they are all intended to relate to the elements, to open to the summer sun and the sea air. While many people retreat to the beach to write, compose music, or paint, most are searching for relaxation and escape from a demanding and complicated urban life.

In this book we show how the most successful seaside decorating has a resort-like feel, where low maintenance, comfort, outdoor meals, and opportunities to unwind and relax are important elements. What are key characteristics of this style? Color is the most important, as it powerfully affects our moods. Probably the most classic beach house palette is blue and white, reflecting the sky and the sand outside. All shades of green or marine blue give the feeling of water, one of the principal elements of nature, which connects a house to the world around it. A sunny yellow, especially in the kitchen, makes a summer morning cheerful. Pink brings in memories of the Caribbean. But don't forget that nothing frames an ocean view like a dazzling all-white room. Add accents of orange or bright blue, and you will have a beautiful space.

With furnishings, you will find that comfortable and practical rattan chairs and side tables evoke broad resort hotel verandas, while sleek outdoor furniture faded to a poetic gray and anything made of driftwood is a great choice for the beach. Worn painted furniture, distressed stainless steel stools, and big, high, draped beds all have a romantic seaside feel. Victorian furniture painted white and nineteenth-century Scandinavian pieces add age and character to any style of beach house.

More time is spent relaxing at a beach house than in town, so it is wise to plan big, deep, comfortable sofas with plenty of pillows. Toss a few sea-themed fabric cushions onto your furniture for a great beachy look. There are lots of terrific nautical-themed textiles available today, including many based on antique seafaring prints. In the bedroom, when hot weather makes it difficult to sleep, you need cool, cotton bedding and soft down pillows. A mosquito net can be a romantic and practical addition to a bed and lend a tropical feel to the room. Think about how to frame your view of the sea, perhaps by hanging transparent, billowing curtains or organic bamboo blinds to filter the sunlight.

There is no room for fussy silks and damasks at the beach. Sun destroys delicate fabrics, and so the best choices are sturdy linens and washable cottons. As a lot of time is spent outdoors, sand, gravel, and even mud are tracked inside, which has to be taken into account when planning furnishings, especially floor coverings. Often it is best to stick with painted wooden floors, terrazzo, or natural fibers like soft flax and sea grass rugs, which absorb damp and add a casual vibe to your rooms.

A beach house offers a wonderful excuse to collect ocean-themed paintings and drawings. These can often be found at local flea markets and antiques shops. Adding wallpaper gives instant character to a new house. There are many nautical themes, including antique maps, anchors, coral, and sailing ships—the list is endless. You can find a wide array of accessories for decorating at the beach. Almost anything found in nature and brought into the house looks great, like driftwood, shells, tree branches, coral, and seedpods. Marine finds like weathered glass bottles, rope, lanterns, maps, hurricane lamps, and antique charts give character to any interior and can all be used in a novel and unexpected manner. Anything gently worn or eroded looks like a beachcombing discovery. Bathrooms become more than just a simple place to bathe—at the beach they are

CLOCKWISE, FROM TOP LEFT: *Decorator Julia Winston's charming house in Sag Harbor, New York. Martyn Lawrence Bullard designed this draped bed for musician Kid Rock's Malibu home. A Carpenter Gothic house owned by Tom Fallon on Shelter Island, New York. Architect Duccio Ermenegildo's bathroom at the beach in Careyes, Mexico.*

constantly in use to wash off sand and clean up after sunbathing. The best sources for bathroom design ideas can be found in resorts and hotels. In recent years, bathrooms have become the focus of a huge hospitality industry. They have evolved into luxurious spalike spaces—for instance, a regular room at the Four Seasons Hotel at Jimbaran Bay, Bali, has four places to bathe, indoors and outside.

When the warm weather gives way to cold wintry evenings with waves pounding outside, a house becomes a defense against the world rather than a place to sit in the embrace of summer. Now it closes up, fires are lit, and another way of life begins. If you choose to live year-round in your beach house or return for weekends throughout the year, you seal your windows against the cold and the focus of the house turns inward. With warm throws over the sofa and heavy duvets on the beds, the house becomes a refuge while other holidaymakers move on. For many, this is the best time of the year—a time when you can have the seaside all to yourself.

There are a lot of great beaches throughout America, and the nearby Caribbean and Mexican coastal regions. To include as wide a range of rooms by the sea as possible, we began with Malibu, where we found Matthew Rolston and Ted Russell's elegantly simple beach house on the sand and antiquarian Richard Shapiro's august Mediterranean villa. South of Los Angeles, Newport Beach was developed as a resort more than a hundred years ago, and here, we show Spencer Croul's small beach cabana, decorated by Peter Dunham. Many holidaymakers are drawn to the white sands of Mexico, and the resort-like property decorated by Martyn Lawrence Bullard, with its thatched palm roofs, is typical of the exclusive Pacific Coast region of Punta Mita.

On America's East Coast, we photographed decoupage artist John Derian's former ship captain's house on Cape Cod, Massachusetts, where a branch of his eponymous New York store is tucked into his garage. We also included Clora Kelly's Shelter Island family home, decorated with great flair and style. We were lucky to run across Chris Mead and Zoë Hoare at Mead's store English Country Antiques in Bridgehampton. He was happy to have us take pictures of his whitewashed eighteenth-century Sagaponack home. Flying down to Florida, we found that many people live by the sea in apartments, such as decorator Juan Montoya in his pied-à-terre in the elegant Helen Mar building in Miami Beach and Simon Doonan and Jonathan Adler in their impossibly chic apartment in the Reef in Palm Beach.

As a tropical retreat, Harbour Island in the Bahamas has been made famous in the design world by India Hicks and David Flint Wood. Their estate-like property has been transformed into a family compound, and we photographed their main home, which was full of children and dogs. New York designer Tom Sheerer has helped many people on the island with their houses, including Olivier and Zoë de Givenchy's beach house—adding another wing and giving it his breezy beach style. He owns a small cottage here with a jaw-dropping kitchen fireplace discovered under planks of wood.

However, you don't have to live by the beach to add these elements of the seaside. Whether you have an apartment or a house in town or in the country, you can take inspiration from many of the homeowners in this book and give your home a feeling of closeness to nature and the ocean even if the sound of the waves is thousands of miles away.

RIGHT: *A large trophy fish dominates Steven Gambrel's Sag Harbor guesthouse fireplace wall.* FOLLOWING SPREAD: *The living room of the eighteenth-century house Chris Mead shares with Zoë Hoare in Sagaponack, New York. The boat is from Mead's collection of early English pond yachts.*

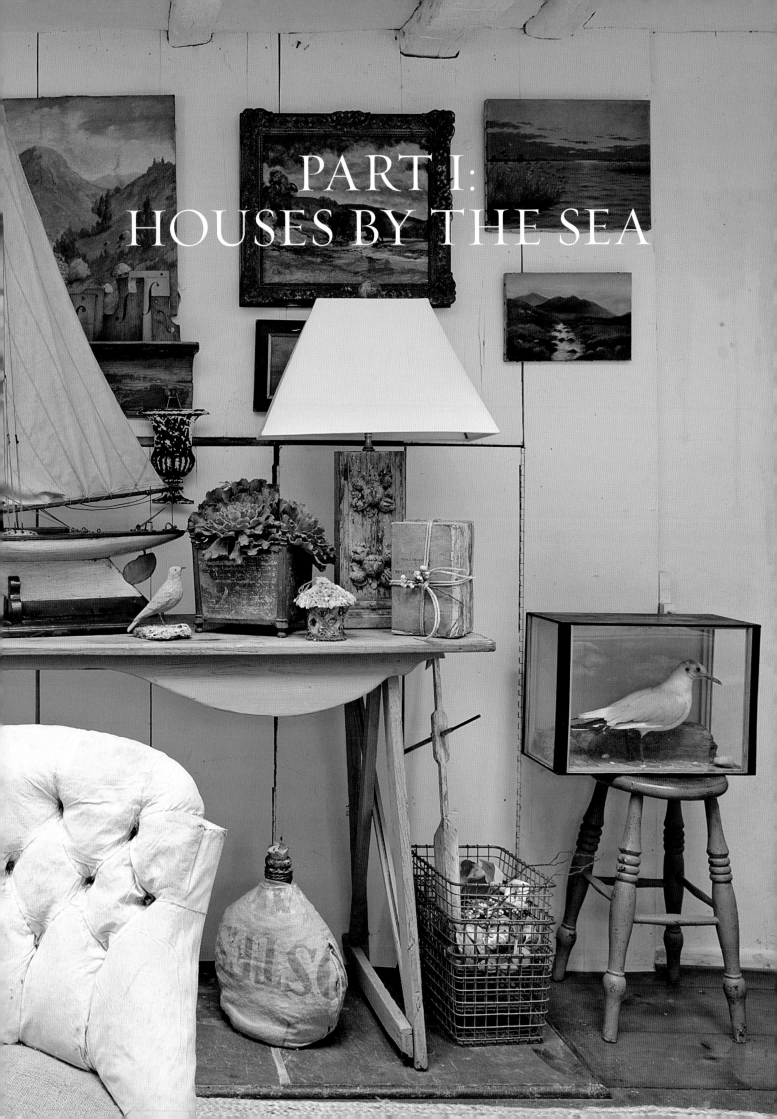

PART I:
HOUSES BY THE SEA

Tropical Style

A BEACH HOUSE BY MARTYN LAWRENCE BULLARD

ALONG THE MEXICAN PACIFIC COAST, the Punta Mita beachside development has at its center the luxurious Four Seasons Hotel, which is surrounded by big private estates that fringe a broad bay. When flying into the nearest airport in Puerto Vallarta, you are immediately hit by a welcome blast of tropical air. After a short twenty-minute drive, you come to a forest of small palm trees that hide the huge beach house built by a Hollywood video entrepreneur nearly six years ago, which has consumed designer Martyn Lawrence Bullard's creative energies for some time. Back then this was a big commission for the decorator, who today has a very successful design company based in Los Angeles, where he works for clients with household names like Elton John, Kid Rock, and Cher. The 40,000-square-foot complex was a challenge to furnish, and Lawrence Bullard began by organizing a shipload of furniture, specifically designed for each room from all over the world, including Indonesia, Turkey, India, and Japan. With fourteen guest rooms, including a separate guesthouse, it would have been easy for the property to feel like a hotel; however, Lawrence Bullard has created individual suites with their own color schemes and furnishings. As he is also a skilled fabric designer, he considered each bed as a different composition of colors, patterns, and textures. Headboards, pillows, bed skirts, and canopies are treated as distinct elements, and Lawrence Bullard mixes and matches fabrics for them with a confident hand from his own range of designs as well as those of his friends, fellow designers Peter Dunham and Carolina Irving.

When you arrive, pathways lined with tropical plantings bring you to a broad entry with a small central fountain inset into the floor. From here passages and flights of stairs lead off to guest quarters, spas, and the private areas of the house, and provide a glimpse of a huge palapa-roofed living room to the ocean beyond. This multipurpose space might have been difficult to decorate. However, it is clearly divided into two parts, with a dining room at one end and, at the other, a lower, larger living space, where Lawrence Bullard designed the furnishings to make the most of the view.

Here, a massive dining table is overhung by a dramatic grouping of huge, festive round lanterns of woven raffia. The space is anchored by a glass-fronted cabinet displaying collections of seashells seemingly collected over a lifetime. The table was created from one huge piece of wood and shipped to Mexico, where twenty people were needed to carry it into the house. This is definitely living on a big scale. Rows of dining chairs upholstered in Lawrence Bullard's Majorelle linen make it clear that big house parties are often taken for granted here, while a smaller round table for more intimate meals at the ocean end of the room has a view of the beach. Here, in another grand gesture the designer has hung a huge overscale Mexican star lamp.

Using his Kaba Kaba linen in blue, Lawrence Bullard designed seating for the living space, which includes a dark blue built-in sofa faced by comfortable armchairs and low Mexican stools, specifically added

Two small fountains cool the air in the entry to the main living area; one is set into a pebbled recess in the floor. The candlestand was designed by Lawrence Bullard.

PREVIOUS SPREAD: *With
a view out to the Pacific
Ocean from the large living
space, Lawrence Bullard
kept the furniture low and
rustic. He included his own
fabrics for the cushions—
Kaba Kaba and Senja.*
RIGHT: *The swimming
pool is aligned with the hot
tub and the ocean.*

LEFT: *The private master bathroom courtyard features a spalike fountain and pool.* RIGHT: *A huge star lamp adds drama to the main outdoor dining table, made from rustic wood. The blue-and-white table settings reflect the colors of the sky and sea.*

so as to not block the view. The various seating areas around the room are united with a large striped rug custom-made by Mansour Modern of Los Angeles.

The master bedroom suite takes up half the ground floor of the main house and includes a well-appointed gym, a spa room, and a bathroom that extends outdoors to a small pool and Jacuzzi in a private courtyard enclosed by a tall wooden fence.

Below, hidden underground, a sybaritic screening room with a bar is furnished with deep sofas and plenty of movies for long summer nights. The two-story guesthouse, with its own outdoor living room, is a short walk across the lawn. Here, Lawrence Bullard has created a more Asian-inspired mood, using tribal wall carvings and many large, comfortable pillows in his Kaba Kaba and Senja fabrics. The large, spacious bedrooms all have an ocean view through the coconut palms, often from their own private balconies.

This is a house designed for entertaining, and the owner customarily arrives for weekends with an entourage of houseguests. He is an unusually dedicated host. By each bedside, a list of services is offered, including round-the-clock massages, saunas, scuba diving, water skiing, and tennis. Using his storehouse of exotic influences, Lawrence Bullard has infused intimacy, comfort, and idiosyncratic detail into a weekend house that is resort-like in scale.

RIGHT: *A long bench designed by Lawrence Bullard occupies a passage that leads to the main house's bedrooms. He used antique Indian textiles for the pillows, and for the seat cushions, a 1940s Mexican Indian blanket found in nearby Puerto Vallarta. Hanging star lamps add a poetic glow. The artworks are by the author.* PAGE 26: *A cabinet filled with shells adds to the decoration of the dining room.* PAGE 27: *Majorelle, a fabric design by Lawrence Bullard, gives the dining chairs a compositional precision. The large hand-colored raffia balls hang weightlessly above the dining table, which was made from one piece of wood and took twenty men to install.*

ABOVE: *The front lanai of the guesthouse is furnished in Lawrence Bullard's fabrics, including sofa cushions in Senja and Kaba Kaba. This is a pleasantly cool place to sit and enjoy an ocean view.* RIGHT: *The Lawrence Bullard–designed armchair is upholstered with his Bodrum Stripe. Added furniture and decorative details are from India and Turkey; they include a wall panel from Southeast Asia.*

LEFT: *A guest bedroom furnished with pillows and a bed canopy, using Peter Dunham's Ikat fabric and a green cashmere throw from Denis Colomb.* ABOVE: *A second upstairs guest bedroom features Lawrence Bullard's Marrakesh fabric on the headboard and pillows. The mirrored side lamps are from the store Hollywood at Home.* PAGE 32: *A vintage Italian side table defines one end of a long corridor. The hanging star lamps were custom made for Lawrence Bullard's line with Troy Lighting.* PAGE 33: *A massage room is a luxurious addition to any beach house. Here, the table is covered by a handwoven Balinese ikat.*

Surf's Up

A BEACH HOUSE BY PETER DUNHAM IN CALIFORNIA

NOT MANY SURFERS BUY A SMALL COTTAGE AT NEWPORT BEACH just to use as a beach cabana—but California is that kind of place. Spencer Croul is a keen surf history buff—he has published many books on the subject, owns a famous collection of early surfboards, and is a cofounder of the Surfing Heritage Foundation. Croul wanted a place that he, his wife Susan, and his two children could use for trips to the beach. Newport Beach was developed in the early twentieth century as a weekend and surfing destination, and the Crouls' house is less than a block from the ocean.

Built in 1915, the small, 850-square-foot cottage needed work. Decorator Peter Dunham, who was working on the Crouls' main house nearby, happily agreed to join architect Scott Laidlaw in what turned into an unexpected amount of restoration. They opened up the ceilings and added tongue-and-groove paneling to the walls. The new floor is reclaimed timber made from train trestles that had fallen into the Salton Sea, a California desert salt lake. It gave them the right period look for the house—Croul claims that at times he can see the salt seeping from the grooves in the boards. They also redid the windows based on the two original windows that they discovered, unchanged, at the back of the house.

Dunham built in as much furniture as he could to save space—he designed a banquette for the dining area of the main room, using fabrics from his own fabric line, and dug up a vintage map, which he turned into a colorful lampshade. The overscale hanging copper lantern, which adds drama to the space, was found by Croul at a ship auction in Florida. Facing this corner is a comfortable living area, where Dunham brought in matching glass-bottle table lamps to give symmetry to the room. He also used his fabric to line and edge the bamboo blinds, providing a subtle decorator touch to the small house. A built-in bunk bed functions as another seating area in a corner of the living room, while the tiny master bedroom is tucked into a separate room next to the kitchen. Here, Dunham's fabrics cover the decorative pillows on the bed. The kitchen, with its commercial-style stove, is fully equipped to prepare food for the hungriest group of beachgoers.

Croul often stops by at the end of the day to go surfing with friends, and this house can double as a guesthouse. As a dedicated beach hangout, this small cottage is a luxury for someone who grew up surfing Newport Beach's "Blackies" surf break and has lived most of his life by the sea.

The Crouls' dining corner was furnished with built-in benches to save space. The cushions are upholstered with fabrics that include Peter Dunham's own Starstruck, St. Tropez, and Arabesque. Spencer Croul bought the large hanging light fitting from a ship sale in Florida.

RIGHT: *The exterior of the 1915 cottage displaying a surfboard from Croul's collection. Cushions on the right of the front porch are in Dunham's Fig Leaf fabric.* FOLLOWING SPREAD: *The living room is a carefully arranged composition of colors and patterns. The armchair at left is upholstered with Dunham's Sheba fabric, and the sofa pillows framing the antique suzani cushion are in his Almont Stripe. Flanking the black-and-white drawings of ships' hulls on the wall is a pair of glass lamps from Dunham's store Hollywood at Home.*

In the kitchen, black-and-white photos of sailboats, found at auction, hang above a pair of raffia stools from Harbinger. A suspended shelf keeps condiments on hand.

ABOVE: *The compact size of the cottage is evident here. A chair upholstered by Dunham in a vintage textile sits below a hanging surfboard from Croul's collection.* RIGHT: *A built-in daybed acts as a second bedroom for Croul's guests. The bed fabric is by Jed Johnson, and the lamp and chair are from Hollywood at Home. The cushions are made with vintage African textiles, while the carpet is vintage Caucasian found at auction. The throw is a hand-spun, handwoven Indian bedcover designed by Dunham.*

The tiny master bedroom is tucked next to the kitchen. The throw cushions are made with Dunham's Globe fabric, while the Euro shams come from John Robshaw.

A Captain's Cabin

TOM SCHEERER'S ISLAND COTTAGE

DESPITE 2011'S HURRICANE IRENE, which was centered over Harbour Island for a very long day and a half ripping up tropical vegetation and shredding palm trees, decorator and architect Tom Scheerer's small, late nineteenth-century "Cash Box" remained intact. Named for the next-door liquor store and sturdily built, this square, stone-walled "box" weathered the storm in true Bahamian style. It helped that the low, two-storied house is located about a block or two away from the seafront. With a guest bedroom upstairs spanning the attic and punctuated by dormer windows, the cottage today is open to the breezes.

This is New York–based Scheerer's second house on the island. The first had been a nearby neglected convent, which he restored more than ten years ago. However, as the rather large building had five bedrooms, Scheerer found himself hosting constant house parties, so he scaled down to three bedrooms when he bought this much smaller house across the road, which was vacant for over twenty years. Including his own properties, Scheerer has designed quite a few houses for friends on the island in the sophisticated casual style that has made him a popular East Coast and Miami decorator. They all show his easy confidence in mixing modern furniture, nineteenth-century furnishings, and bright, colorful fabrics. Scheerer's main inspiration is the clarity and focus of the work of such master designers as Billy Baldwin and David Hicks.

The front door, made of latticed wood, lets air flow through the house via a passage that leads to two bedrooms and a bathroom on the ground floor and an open back loggia, which Scheerer added to extend the living space and to take advantage of the tropical climate. This is a breezy space with one side walled in by open slatted screens, sheltered from the noise of the street. He spends much of his time here, with two outdoor sofas and rattan rocking chairs set on a circular mat right next to the kitchen. Nearby in the garden at the rear of the house Scheerer built an outdoor shower inside a tall, boxy structure to stop sand from being trekked indoors.

Dominated by a spectacular open fireplace, the kitchen was once a separate structure. When Scheerer found the property several years ago, it was lined in pink-painted plywood and used as a storage space for the liquor store next door. He noticed it had a chimney and stripped the walls to reveal one of

In the aqua-blue-painted attic Scheerer has hung a collection of seashells decoratively encased in plaster.

ABOVE: *The house Cash Box opens directly onto the street. Here, you can see the central passage that directs cool sea breezes through the house.* RIGHT: *Scheerer's trademark in the tropics is the use of inventively scrolling bentwood chairs.*

The porch that Scheerer added to the back of the house works well as an outdoor sitting room. Facing the garden, it is a comfortable place to entertain friends, furnished as it is with curved bamboo rocking chairs and a pair of sofas with cushions made with John Robshaw fabric.

LEFT: *A print depicting the nearby island of New Providence, by Winslow Homer, hangs on a bedroom wall.* RIGHT: *A pair of signature bentwood chairs and a pair of sconces, designed by Scheerer, flank a living room cabinet filled with books and shells.*

the strongest features of the house—a fireplace where, in the nineteenth century, all the family meals had been cooked. A new floor of Cuban concrete patterned tiles came next. The kitchen proved large enough to accommodate a drop-leaf leaf table and Scheerer's signature bentwood chairs. He linked it to the main house by a small passage, which he lined with shelves to serve as a butler's pantry.

A small, cozy sitting room, which has been cleverly shoehorned into the stair landing, is furnished with a tall glass-fronted cabinet holding books and such beachcombing finds as shells. Steps lead up to the attic, where under the roof, Scheerer moved a wall back and added a second bathroom with a large white bathtub. (When he bought the house it had no indoor plumbing.) This extra space gave him the opportunity to design a striking bedroom, centered with a white-draped four-poster bed. He painted both rooms a glorious aqua blue that gave the attic an unexpected unity.

The exterior of the house got new windows with gray shutters and a coat of whitewash. With the house right on the street, surrounded by the sounds of roosters and chickens and open to breezes from the beach, Scheerer is enveloped by the island as soon as he arrives. Happily, having plenty of work in Miami and nearby Nassau means Scheerer gets to visit his charmingly compact beach house filled with collections of rocks, shells, and books almost every other month.

ABOVE: *Shelves in the outdoor living room have been added to display finds from the sea as well as useful household supplies.* RIGHT: *The kitchen was once a separate building. Here, you can see how Scheerer joined it to the main house with a small passage, which he uses as a butler's pantry. On the floor are concrete tiles from Cuba.* FOLLOWING SPREAD: *The old concrete and brick fireplace dominates the kitchen. When he bought the house, the ceiling had already been opened up. Scheerer refinished the walls and painted them white. A small table sits at one side of the room for meals.*

ABOVE: *Scheerer opened up the attic—painting all of it aqua blue—and added a central, draped bed. Dormer windows provide light and fresh sea air.* RIGHT: *By moving a wall back, Scheerer was able to add a bathroom with vintage fixtures to the upstairs space.*

Shipshape

CHRIS MEAD AND ZOË HOARE IN SAGAPONACK

WHEN ZOË HOARE WAS ON HOLIDAY FROM LONDON and visiting friends in the Hamptons, she wasn't looking for a new life. But when she met British photographer and store owner Chris Mead at a Long Island dinner party one night four years ago, little did she realize that she would be living and working in a very different part of the world within the year. Hoare started selling antiques in her native Australia while working for her mother, noted English antiques dealer Appley Hoare. She and her mother moved together to London in the mid-1990s, where she opened a flower shop next to Appley Hoare Antiques.

The couple shares many enthusiasms and interests, which happily include an eighteenth-century saltbox Mead had bought a few years earlier. Set in the picturesque Hamptons beachside town of Sagaponack (which was called "Sagg" when it was founded in 1653), their property was first used for potato farming. Called the Topping-Hedges House, Mead's beach house was one of many historic early homes in this part of Long Island and had survived relatively unchanged. He had been looking for a place not far from the larger of his two Hamptons stores, English Country Antiques, and having helped produce numerous books on American country style, Mead knew how he wanted this charming small property to look. Despite being everyone's favorite house in the area, most people were afraid to do the interior work needed to make it more up-to-date.

Mead stripped the house back to its components, whitewashed it, and opened up part of the ceiling in the main room to reveal existing skylights. Today the rooms glow all year long. When Hoare moved in, he reworked an area behind the old front door to act as a wardrobe for her clothing; otherwise very little else was needed. They have happily followed their enthusiasms—decorating this house, despite its Colonial American origins, in a breezy and casual international style that would look equally at home in the South of France or Ibiza.

Hidden behind a row of trees, the compact old shingled house sits in a large open garden, anchored by impressive specimen trees. Like a storybook cottage, it is fringed with flowering hydrangeas. The main entry opens into the long living space, which includes sitting room, kitchen, and dining room decorated with the couple's collections. At this end hangs a row of vintage hand mirrors above a tabletop display of hat stands. The rest of the space is filled with nautical references like sailing ships, seagulls, seashells, and other treasures.

Of course having thousands of square feet of furniture store space nearby to "borrow" from makes decorating decisions for the couple easier than for most of us, but comfort is also the key here. Mali, their venerable Staffordshire bull terrier, is difficult to pry from the sofas, but their easy-care linen slipcovers are not

RIGHT: *A pair of bicycles used for trips to the beach waits outside the front door of the shingled eighteenth-century house.* FOLLOWING SPREAD: *Mead opened up a section of the sitting room ceiling to add light to the lower floor of the house. With white slipcovers on the sofas and sturdy sea-grass matting, the room is designed for comfortable seaside living.*

CLOCKWISE, FROM TOP LEFT: *Mead collects English seaside paintings, which hang behind a pond yacht flanked by matching table lamps. A boxed sea bird from English Country Antiques adds to the theme of beach life in the living room. Vintage French blue-and-white fabric cushions match a collection of glazed French pots in the sitting room. Twigs inventively fixed to the wall act as hooks for bags and baskets.* RIGHT: *In the entry, a collection of hat stands and hand mirrors anchored by a vintage dog painting attests to the couple's skill in displaying their various finds.*

A well-worn nineteenth-
century European daybed
sits in front of the upstairs
master bedroom fireplace.
The pillows are made with
vintage French fabrics.

LEFT: *The kitchen and dining end of the main living space are warmed by a black cast-iron stove. A collection of vintage napkins from Hoare's website lies on the dining table.* RIGHT: *In a sunny corner of the room, a collection of succulents and a pair of wooden candelabra sit on a corner table.*

hard to maintain. At the other end of the space, the kitchen appliances and sink line up inconspicuously, designed to blend in with the rest of the room. The master bedroom, where the couple has furnished the bed with colorful John Robshaw textiles, leads off this central part of the house. An ancient chimneypiece adds character to the bedroom; the fireplaces are closed up, as they have yet to be restored.

Upstairs, the open walkway, which feels like a galley in an old sailing ship, leads to two well-appointed guest bedrooms. Here the beachside feeling is continued with cool, minty colors and fabrics in nautical stripes. Steps continue upward past the whitewashed bulk of the chimney to the attic, which is Mead's workspace while he is at home. However, he can often be found downstairs, taking calls at the kitchen table, which has a view outside to the garden. Here on long summer evenings, the couple regularly entertains outdoors at a large weathered table with fresh produce bought from the vegetable stand next door.

The house has kept its integrity as an old building, thanks to Mead's understanding of how its ancient timbers contribute to the structure. He has left most of them exposed and carefully kept paneled walls, using gallons of flat white paint to tie the house together, which gives it a fresh and clean feel. Blue-and-white fabrics and china look wonderful here, and their simple charm, along with the couple's personal collections, make the house a comfortable home.

ABOVE: *Open kitchen shelves are a great way to display china and glass.* RIGHT: *The upstairs passage to the bedrooms looks like the inside of an old sailing ship. It opens to the sitting room below. The architectural details are unified with several coats of whitewash.*

LEFT: *The guest bedroom linens are from John Robshaw. Suitcases can be left on the vintage bench at the foot of the iron bed.* ABOVE, CLOCKWISE, FROM TOP LEFT: *A casual chair in the corner of the master bedroom. The master bed is covered in John Robshaw linens. A striped armchair in an upstairs bedroom. One of a pair of guest beds in the same room.*

ABOVE: *Hoare's mother, antiquarian Appley Hoare, when visiting from England, designed a display of buckets and pots at the back of the house.* RIGHT: *In summer, the couple entertains often on the back terrace, conveniently placed next to the kitchen door. This dining area looks onto a large garden, which surrounds the house.*

Ship Ahoy

JOHN DERIAN ON CAPE COD

SUCCESSFUL SHOPKEEPER AND PRODUCT DESIGNER JOHN DERIAN'S IMPASSIONED QUEST for raw material for his decoupage designs evokes the pursuits of Victorian-era collectors. His particular vision, apparent to all of us familiar with his decoupage images of plants and animals, was distilled from childhood experiences and later refined at art school. He made his first "repeatable" decoupage plate in 1989, and New York's home accessories store Lexington Gardens took his work in 1990. Just two years later he opened his own first shop on East Second Street in downtown Manhattan. Derian's success lies in his ability to tap into a collective nostalgia for nineteenth-century prints and related aesthetics, creating a way to isolate images that are humble, iconic, and quirky and printing them onto simple glass plates and decorative objects. His life revolves around a continued search for imagery from the past, ideas, and stimulation.

The 1789 ship captain's house, of which he is only the third owner, in Provincetown, Massachusetts, is Derian's residence when he is not in New York. One of his major discoveries, it fits his lifestyle like a well-worn glove. Massachusetts-born Derian first visited the seaside resort of Provincetown on childhood holidays. Located at the far end of Cape Cod, it has been a resort town since the early twentieth century. Provincetown was settled by the British in 1727 and became a whaling center in the nineteenth century. Today the town's center is listed on the National Register of Historic Places, and summer residents have included Tennessee Williams, Norman Mailer, Robert Motherwell, and more recently, director John Waters.

Six years ago Derian noticed a For Sale sign on this dilapidated but pretty Colonial house on a lane that is one of Provincetown's busy main thoroughfares. From the Greek Revival porch there was a clear view of the harbor, with a short walk to the beach. When he first stepped into the house, the experience took his breath away. The interior was largely original and unrestored, with peeling paint and charmingly distressed 1930s wallpaper. Floorboards were expansively wide, always a winning feature in early New England houses, while door and window moldings had the delicacy of detailing rare in modern houses, with handles and locks both small and simple in design. Two sets of double doors in the main rooms added quirky charm.

Now the house appears remarkably unchanged, and at first glance it looks as if he has done little beyond sweeping the floor. Derian was unwilling to touch the peeling paint and faded 1930s wallpaper, and has made the preexisting patina the primary decorative theme of the house. In places the wallpaper has been stripped away to reveal a rough plaster surface underneath—its organic finish composed of plaster, horsehair, and crushed seashells. Behind the scenes, the house's electricity and plumbing have been fixed and the five chimneys rebuilt. In the kitchen, which looks like an old school room, there are new appliances and the floor has been painted. The sitting room sets the stage for the rest of the house. With wallpaper and painted wainscoting, the look is comfortable and undecorated, perfect for a relaxed seaside house where swimming, bicycle riding, and Scrabble are the main pursuits. Nineteenth-century armchairs and couches, some from his own Hepplewhite-style

In an upstairs sitting room, a nineteenth-century sofa displaying vintage textiles overlooks the sea. The walls have been left unpainted.

LEFT: *The restored 1789 sea captain's house seen from the beach. The Greek Revival columns were added in the early nineteenth century. Tim Callis, Derian's garden designer, planted the front with native bayberry.*
RIGHT: *A back porch is used for outdoor dining. Rustic beams used as stools surround a marble-topped metal table. A forest of European onion lanterns hangs above.*

collection and in various stages of re-upholstering, are friendly and inviting and covered with overscale cushions, brightly patterned to complement the wallpaper. The venerable Skip, who is now nearly seventeen years old and looks like an old ship's cat, can often be found asleep here in the afternoons. Windows are left open to allow the constant sea breeze to filter through. No need for elaborate flower arrangements and stiff side tables here. In the dining room, patterns come into play again, the toile cloth covering the early 1880s table echoing the floral theme of the wallpaper. The dining chairs come from the Brimfield Flea Market.

Derian loves to entertain—the six bedrooms upstairs, some of which are located in a newer addition from the 1840s at the back, are constantly occupied on weekends by friends visiting from New York and elsewhere. Reached by a pair of staircases, the rooms on the upper floor almost all have a view of the ocean, and a small landing, furnished as a sitting area, acts as a central gathering space watched over by a pair of black-inked bird drawings.

Below, in the newer wing, Derian has installed a shop, a smaller version of his New York stores that gives him an extra reason to spend time here. The designer swims daily year-round, although he concedes that in the winter it is only for a few seconds. During the summer Derian enjoys looking back at the house from the water and being reminded that it once belonged to a sea captain.

One of several sitting rooms where Derian has carefully left the walls unrestored. This gives his house character and a poetic atmosphere, which he adds to with elements from nature, such as the sponge on the chimneypiece and the bushy dried plant on the right.

ABOVE: *The unusual double doors lead into the central dining room. The wallpaper has been left in its original condition.* RIGHT: *Antique dining chairs from Belgium surround a table covered in a vintage French toile. A built-in glass-fronted cabinet holds glassware and finds from the beach.*

CLOCKWISE, FROM TOP LEFT: *A view into the upstairs front sitting room from the landing. A rectangle of vintage stretched linen adds a romantic touch to the peeling wallpaper. Tumbleweed fills an unused fireplace. A nineteenth-century painting evokes the spirit of the sea captain who built the house.* RIGHT: *A nineteenth-century portrait of a boy and his dog overlooks John Derian's Cove sofa in the ground-floor front living room.*

ABOVE: *A nineteenth-century white wicker table holds food and utensils in the kitchen.* RIGHT: *The age of the house is obvious in the front entry. Stairs lead up to the bedrooms.* FOLLOWING SPREAD: *In the kitchen, Derian updated the appliances, painted the floor white, and added a central nineteenth-century round butcher-block table from Paula Rubenstein in New York. A Mennonite mirror shade from Robert Ogden hangs above. An uncovered nineteenth-century sofa provides a place mainly for Skip the cat to watch the kitchen activities.*

ABOVE: *In a front bedroom, a maple canopy bed from the 1830s is covered with a vintage throw by Jeanette Farrier. On the wall is a nineteenth-century Dutch seascape.* RIGHT: *A Hugo Guinness drawing hangs near the bedroom fireplace.*

CLOCKWISE, FROM TOP LEFT: *A sunny upstairs guest bedroom. A nineteenth-century portrait gazes confidently at the viewer in place of a powder room mirror. Despite flying in from New York with Derian, Skip, his venerable cat, looks as if he has spent his life at sea. A lobster print hangs on the wall of Derian's bedroom.* RIGHT: *Hugo Guinness's linocut* Chrysanthemum *leans against the wall in an upstairs guest bedroom. A nineteenth-century gilded American mirror adds a formal touch above the convenient sink.*

Island Time

OLIVIER AND ZOË DE GIVENCHY IN THE BAHAMAS

ACROSS A BROAD LAWN AND PAST A LARGE BANYAN TREE, you enter the de Givenchy house through a breezeway where a long table is sociably set up for a meal. The breezeway connects the two wings of the building, which were reworked from a single structure by New York decorator Tom Scheerer, in consultation with Olivier de Givenchy, who works as a private banker in faraway London. Here is how a house in the Bahamas should be: welcoming and airy, with plenty of ceiling fans, bright colors, and lots of hospitality.

Several years ago while Olivier was out with friends, including Scheerer, who lives nearby, he was shown this property, with its distant views of the harbor. Rumor has it that the swimming pool was built in the 1950s for use by the Duke and Duchess of Windsor while he was governor of the Bahamas. On this unusually large lot of land in town (about two acres), de Givenchy and Scheerer kept the pool's shape but rebuilt the surrounding house to accommodate children and the constant flow of houseguests, adding a large kitchen for entertaining. Scheerer had already worked on several other houses on the island, including two of his own, and understands how to decorate for a tropical climate, as well as what was possible on an island, where everything arrives via ferry.

For Scheerer, working with Olivier was a flashback to his past in Paris, where, quite by chance, he had found himself decorating for de Givenchy's uncle, the couturier Hubert de Givenchy. He hastens to add that he only followed the lead of the great designer. Here, on Harbour Island, Scheerer brought a sophisticated New York look to de Givenchy's nephew's tropical island house, using bright, colorful fabrics from Schumacher and Quadrille and cheerful patterned tile in the kitchen, and paneling the library with "faux-driftwood." Scheerer furnished the living room with a pair of facing sofas, and added rattan chairs for a relaxed beach feel. The fireplace is used in winter and is a strong focal point of the room. The dining table in the corner is often used for family meals.

A useful latticed gazebo was retained, but everything else was reconfigured, including the interior rooms, and every window and door was replaced. Scheerer designed a large sitting room, the library, and a guestroom suite, which has a view of the pool. The stylishly high headboard of the guest bed was created by the simple expedient of stacking three normal-size headboards one above another. Furnished like another living room, and enlivened with a large Indian hanging, an outdoor alcove facing the pool takes advantage of the warm air of the tropics.

A decoupage plate from John Derian
adds a tropical note next to the palm leaf
on the sitting room mantelpiece.

Connected by the breezeway, the new two-story building considerably expanded the property and provided the top floor with ocean views. Bedrooms for Olivier's two children were part of the brief, as well as a large master bedroom upstairs overlooking the harbor. Olivier designed the four-poster bed, which is hung with a gauzy fabric.

Recently Olivier and his Australian wife, Zoë, got married at the picturesque pink-painted local church, which was a chance for their many friends to fly in and enjoy the famous blue sea and pink beaches of the island. The house, with its open-air dining room and spacious surrounding garden, was the perfect backdrop for the event. Happily, the couple manages to get here quite often, as flying to Harbour Island adds only a few short hours onto a business trip to New York.

ABOVE: *The new wing of the house overlooks the pool, rumored to have been used by the Duke and Duchess of Windsor while he was governor of the Bahamas.* RIGHT: *A grouping of baskets by the kitchen door holds a supply of sandals and beach accessories. The eighteenth-century Chinese table and mirror add a formal simplicity.* FOLLOWING SPREAD: *The central breezeway dining room is open to the elements. A long table made of pecky cypress extends for large dinner parties. Scheerer designed the mirrored copper wall sconces, and the baskets hold table supplies and beach accessories.*

ABOVE: *A row of candles separated by a variety of collected seashells gives the dining table an island feel.* RIGHT: *Red-painted branches imitating coral give a note of contrast to the open dining room shelving. Beach towels in baskets are handy for a trip to the seaside.* FOLLOWING SPREAD: *The sitting room has a cool, breezy quality. Scheerer chose rattan chairs to give a note of informality to the space. He relacquered the cylindrical tables and covered the cushions with China Seas fabrics from Quadrille. At Christmas, the evenings are cool enough to use the fireplace.*

ABOVE: *Scheerer paneled the library with faux driftwood to give a beachside feel to the room. The bookcases are suspended white boxes, ideal for displaying shell collections.* RIGHT: *The library doubles as a media room, so comfortable sofas were added for watching television.* FOLLOWING SPREAD: *The outdoor seating alcove, which faces the pool, is backed by a dramatic hanging from India. This would be an easy addition to any house, as it provides shelter as well as a comfortable place to hang out.*

RIGHT: *This bedroom, designed for Olivier's daughter, is one of the most dramatic rooms in the house. The canopies are fixed to the ceiling, and the extravagant driftwood lamp reduces the formality of the height of the space.* PAGE 110: *The master bathroom continues the driftwood theme. Scheerer designed the wall sconces.* PAGE 111: *The dramatic guest bed was created from three normal-size headboards fastened to the wall. The bed skirt fabric is from Schumacher.*

Malibu Mediterranean

RICHARD SHAPIRO'S BROAD BEACH VILLA

WALK DOWN THE GRAVEL PATH of designer and antiquarian Richard Shapiro's house by the sea and you will feel as if you have left Malibu and been transported to an exotic part of the windswept Mediterranean coast. Lined with pencil-thin cypress trees, clipped, rounded plants, and antique columns, the path leads to an enigmatic seventeenth-century wooden front door. An arch on the left opens to a small, tiled courtyard, where a patterned Moroccan fountain adds an extra note to the distant sound of the ocean waves. Shapiro has designed the main sea view to reveal itself slowly. As you continue through the door, the magnificent height of the ceiling provides a moment's pause, and then the ocean appears—stretching to infinity through huge floor-to-ceiling metal-framed windows.

It is a tribute to Shapiro's skill as a designer that this does not look like a new house—it was finished just a short year or so ago. Like his main house in Los Angeles, he brought in as many elements as he could to give the impression of great antiquity, including huge, imported rustic beams installed by crane and a large seventeenth-century Cypriot stone fireplace, which gives a focus to the sitting room. Above this, adding a note of luxury in the midst of all these raw materials, is a seventeenth-century gilt-wood mirror. Shapiro dressed the large set of facing armchairs in white linen and kept the rest of the furniture white to give the room a dreamy, open quality. The 150-year-old cypress tree framing the ocean view looks as though it had been placed there by central casting. However, this helped Shapiro in his decision to buy the property, as the tree makes the house look as if it is on the Italian coast, albeit carved out of a much older wing of an aristocratic 1930s villa.

Next to the entry, a sharply curving staircase with an unexpectedly architectural banister winds up to the open master bedroom on the mezzanine level, where a bed has been carefully positioned to capture the view through the sitting room windows to the crashing waves below. Here, the frescoes by Russian artist Ilia Anossov that run around the entire room can be seen up close; these, along with the plaster walls, give the mezzanine an almost ancient sensibility. A nineteenth-century Uzbek suzani is draped over the bed. Beneath this space is a library, which doubles as a more intimately scaled second

The 150-year-old Monterey cypress, native to California,
inspired the Mediterranean style of the house, as
it reminded Shapiro of trees in that part of the world.

ABOVE: *The seventeenth-century Italian front door opens to a collection of antique garden elements, including a nineteenth-century English amphora. These pieces add a feeling of antiquity to the garden.* RIGHT: *A dramatic curving staircase, with its steel balustrade, leads to the bedroom mezzanine.*

ABOVE: *The gravel path to the front door is landscaped with clipped bushes, orange trees, and Mediterranean cypress trees.* RIGHT: *Shapiro designed the Moroccan-inspired concrete staircase that descends to the beach.*

sitting room. A smaller, checkered stone tile covers the floor, and another Cypriot stone fireplace anchors the room. A large square ottoman covered by a textile from Istanbul, and others from Iran and Turkey, add richness to the space. A gilded eighteenth-century Spanish mirror hangs over a broad sofa on the opposite wall.

Outside, Shapiro has made the most of the narrow lot's space by creating outdoor seating areas that overlook the ocean view. At the side of the house he has installed a small outdoor fireplace where he and his friend, artist Patricia Roach, light a fire on cool summer nights at the end of the day and sit with a glass of wine to enjoy the evening sea breezes.

ABOVE: *A mirror from Shapiro's furniture company, Studiolo, hangs over a seventeenth-century Italian carved keystone in a sheltered corner of the outdoor side terrace.* RIGHT: *The large seventeenth-century gilt-wood mirror hanging above the Cypriot chimneypiece from the same period contrasts with the faded concrete tones of the dramatic main living space. Shapiro designed the large armchairs and added nineteenth-century Ghanaian footstools. The white-painted cast-bronze floor lamp on the right is by artist Patricia Roach.*

ABOVE AND RIGHT: *In the library, overlooked by an eighteenth-century Spanish mirror, textiles from Iran and Turkey decorate the long sofa and ottoman. A comfortable sofa in the corner is upholstered with vintage striped fabric, and a small fifteenth-century table holds books.*

LEFT: *Hanging on the wall of the main living space is a pair of sixteenth-century Cosmatesque-style floor panels, excavated in Malta. The dining table is Tense by MDF Italia; Shapiro designed the matching bench seat.* ABOVE: *A group of wicker chairs and a mid-century red-painted small table face an outdoor fireplace. The cushions are covered in vintage red-striped fabrics.*

ABOVE: *The height of the main room seen from the bedroom mezzanine gives it drama on a large scale. Here, you can see the grouping of tables and chairs, which facilitates the mixed use of the space. Shapiro had the stone tiles cut, and deliberately chipped, to add an antique patina to the floor.* RIGHT: *Near the kitchen, a vintage glass Waterfall table by Pace sits in front of a linen-covered sofa custom-fitted to the alcove.*

ABOVE: *A small courtyard separates the main house from a guesthouse over the garage.* RIGHT: *The Moroccan-tiled fountain is a striking feature of this space, adding a gentle sound of water to the path by the front door.* FOLLOWING SPREAD: *The mezzanine that serves as the master bedroom overlooks the large living room and sea beyond the tall two-story windows. The bedspread is a nineteenth-century Uzbek suzani, while a seventeenth-century Italian Savonarola chair sits nearby.*

Tropical Living

JUAN MONTOYA IN MIAMI BEACH

A TRUE COSMOPOLITAN, DECORATOR JUAN MONTOYA OWNS APARTMENTS AROUND THE WORLD, including New York, Paris, Bogotá, and this exotic Miami Beach apartment, which he shares with his partner, Urban Karlsson. Here, you can see how he has ingeniously transformed a small two-room pied-à-terre into a richly decorated space that feels larger than it really is. It is quite a contrast to the sprawling country house on 110 acres of forested hills that he and Karlsson share in upstate New York.

In 1994 Montoya bought this apartment in the Art Deco district of Miami's South Beach in the historic seven-story Helen Mar building, which fronts on a canal and has a view of the ocean. The legendary swim star Esther Williams owned the penthouse in the 1930s. During the 1990s, Miami was all about color and nightlife, and Montoya decorated his rooms to reflect this. Built as two studios and then joined together at a later date, Montoya refined the apartment by linking the two main rooms with the kitchen. Since then the city has become more sophisticated, with new buildings by architects Frank Gehry and Herzog & de Meuron, and it now yearly hosts Art Basel Miami Beach. This spurred Montoya to redecorate in 2003 using muted colors and more organic materials. The kitchen has recently been redone with gleaming white cabinets and is veiled from the living space with a dark lattice screen, which makes the rooms seem more mysterious and indefinable.

Today, unexpectedly large objects like a millstone imported from Thailand and an overscale eighteenth-century armoire from China are combined with small, delicate sculptures and soft fabrics to give depth and contrast to the sitting room. Great decorators like Montoya are more like sculptors in the way they use shapes, surfaces, and materials. Often in the rooms they design they employ antiques and artifacts from other cultures to create compositions on tabletops or on top of armoires to humanize and play with scale. The first glimpse of this apartment, upon opening the front door, is a carefully composed arrangement of shapes—a large, fluted white cement urn sits on a column of wood from the Philippines in front of a black, white, and gray abstract painting by Montoya himself, which completes the tableau. A large painting of African figures by Hugo Bastidas adds extra dimension to the nearby wall, and an African-inspired frieze running just below the white-painted ceiling unifies the space. The dining table, made from an Indonesian bowling alley floor, sits where the windows meet at a corner, giving it a view across the watery canal and the ocean beyond. Looking like an opera set, speedboats bob near a small arched pedestrian bridge.

The master bedroom is painted a cozy dark brown with a white ceiling, which gives it added height. Here, Montoya has kept to a calm palette except for the introduction of a purple artwork by Karen

RIGHT: *A collection of walking sticks found in Malaysia is kept in a carved antique architectural element by the front door.* FOLLOWING SPREAD: *The Art Deco Helen Mar apartment building overlooks a canal near the oceanfront. A bridge leads to the beach.*

PREVIOUS SPREAD: *A painting by Hugo Bastidas makes the sitting room seem bigger with its photolike three-dimensional realism. Cambodian cane chairs face a comfortable grouping of chairs and a large sofa. The oval side tables were designed by Montoya.* ABOVE, CLOCKWISE, FROM TOP LEFT: *On one side of the living room Montoya has installed a dark open screen, which closes to hide the kitchen. In the kitchen, a group of Chinese figures sits on top of a nineteenth-century pharmacy cabinet from Sri Lanka. A water wheel on the bedroom table veils the window and gives the room a sense of privacy. An Indian jali screens a kitchen window next to the drinks tray.* RIGHT: *A careful composition greets the visitor upon opening the front door. Astor lies by a decorative plaster ball in front of a 1970s monochromatic painting by Montoya. A 1930s cement urn sits on a wood base from the Philippines.*

Butler Connell above the bed. As in all his rooms, the walls are covered in paintings, prints, and drawings, and include a mixed-media work by Louise Bourgeois. The furnishings are in shades of white, which provide a contrast to the moody colors of the rest of the space. The trellis motif of the previous room is repeated in the doors to the master bathroom and closet. An unexpectedly large water wheel dominates a table in front of the window, and provides privacy as well as drama to the bedroom.

Montoya and Karlsson often fly to Miami with their small white dog, Astor, to work on various decorating projects. Luckily when work is finished they can go home to this comfortable and elegant small apartment with the warm tropical beach only a short few blocks away.

ABOVE: *A huge millstone from Thailand adds drama to the dining corner of the apartment. The African-inspired frieze around the room unifies the space.* RIGHT: *Resembling an opera or movie set, the view from the sitting room looks across the canal to the sea.*

The dark brown walls of the bedroom are given a lift by the crisp white palette used elsewhere throughout this room. A blue-and-white-striped dhurrie rug adds another color note, as does the Karen Butler Connell painting above the bed. The white-framed red string assemblage on the left is by Louise Bourgeois.

140

Coastal Contemporary

MATTHEW ROLSTON AND TED RUSSELL IN MALIBU

ANYONE WHO HAS PICKED UP A MAGAZINE OR TURNED ON THE TELEVISION in the last twenty years will have seen unforgettable glossy images of movie stars and rock musicians by photographer Matthew Rolston that live in our collective visual history. He normally specializes in a certain type of beauty that is a direct inheritance from old Hollywood glamour photography—evident in his print and television campaigns for L'Oréal, Revlon, Gap, Polo Ralph Lauren, and Clairol—and certainly needs a place when he can get a weekend or two to escape from the pressure this kind of work demands.

With his partner, decorator Ted Russell, Rolston recently bought a beach house in Malibu, not far from their home in Trousdale, an elegantly modern corner of Beverly Hills. Their city home had been designed by mid-century architect Rex Lottery in 1966 and featured in the March 2011 Hollywood issue of *Vanity Fair* as the previous home of Johnny Carson producer Freddie de Cordova. It is the center of a glamorous movie-land lifestyle, and continuing in this tradition, Malibu seemed the right choice for a beach retreat, especially as it is only a short hour or so away. As the most desirable locations in Malibu are set back on roads leading from the noisy and busy Pacific Coast Highway, where houses are suspended over the water, like lake houses, Rolston and Russell acted quickly when they found this place for sale near one they had been renting for some years. Part of a development from the 1950s, it had evolved over the years into a rather fussy old-fashioned beach house, which took some time to rework. The couple brought in an architect who had previously worked on the house to streamline the interior spaces and upgrade the finishes and surfaces, especially in the main living room, which also includes the kitchen and a dining area.

As soon as you open the front door, the view from the entry extends through the living room out to the usually calm water of the Pacific Ocean beyond a small glassed-in terrace. At once the distant traffic noise recedes and a more peaceful atmosphere prevails. To keep the mood tranquil, Russell and Rolston stuck to a cream and black palette throughout the airy space, adding carefully curated finds from their many travels abroad. Russell explains that in the year and a half before they moved in, they were collecting ideas from resorts in Bali, Bangkok, and Cambodia. Another big influence was from the North Island in the Seychelles, where a favorite resort used natural elements like tree trunks and driftwood in its furnishings.

The couple acted as each other's client. Rolston is also interested in design, having recently consulted on the Redbury, a new Hollywood hotel, and he has always been very involved in the sets for his various

Outdoor furniture by John Hutton is covered in faux fur throws during the cool Malibu evenings. Clear tempered-glass balcony walls shelter this outdoor living room from the sea breezes and enable views up the California coast.

LEFT: *The front gate leads into the house and directly to the sea.* RIGHT: *From the front deck, the sea looks deceptively calm. Rolston finds this chaise a comfortable place to relax on the weekends.*

photo and video shoots. The couple gave each other presents for the house before they moved in, which are carefully placed around the various rooms. For the main space, Russell ebonized a tree trunk–like dining table base, found in nearby Santa Barbara, which he surrounded with comfortable white-upholstered banquettes. Two matching white sofas face each other at the other end of the room in front of a fireplace. The nearby master bedroom has a cozy draped bed and plenty of mirrors to reflect the ocean so this jewel-like room has an abundance of light. In addition to two bedrooms, leading from the large master bathroom is a small workspace for Russell, as he often has clients at the beach. Every room is carefully lit at night. Lighting is one of Rolston's specialties as a photographer and director, and in his own house he has spent time making it subtle and inconspicuous.

Practical stone floors run throughout the house, cleverly disguising trails of tracked-in sand amd seamlessly flowing outside to the deck. Here, much time is spent relaxing and looking out to the ocean. This area is furnished like an outdoor living room, with glass railings and fur throws, as evenings in Malibu—even in the summer—can be quite cool. Rolston does not seem to mind that through the large plate-glass windows, when the sea becomes just a horizontal line against the sky, the view looks just like the television screens he has left behind in the studio.

CLOCKWISE, FROM TOP LEFT: *A collection of seashells and coral enlivens a dining room shelf. Daisy sits by the front door on a white slipcovered chair next to an African stool. On top of a table from Mecox Gardens rests a lifelike bronze crab. A Javanese textile hangs above a long boatlike tray, which sits on one of two benches from Hudson Furniture.* RIGHT: *The main living space includes two seating groups and a dining area at the far end. To keep to a monochromatic palette, two Ashanti stools were given a coat of white automotive paint. The rug is from Morocco.*

Island Life

INDIA HICKS AND DAVID FLINT WOOD ON HARBOUR ISLAND

MANY FAMILIES WITH BEACH HOUSES IN EXOTIC PLACES MANAGE THE ILLUSION of a carefree idle life for several weeks in summer, which lasts right up to the plane ride home. However, India Hicks has become the embodiment of the idea of tropical escape—retreating from the everyday world to create her own version of paradise with her partner, David Flint Wood, and their children, who run barefoot over Harbour Island when they are not in boarding school back in England. To see a picture of a young, long-haired, blonde mother with a child leaning against a coconut palm tree is to immediately think of India Hicks. The couple's best-selling book, *Island Life*, showed us that it is possible to leave the "real world" behind and live happily ever after.

While Hicks holidayed as a child on nearby Eleuthera with her father, the legendary decorator David Hicks, Flint Wood arrived in 1995 to help run a local hotel. He left a career behind in London in an advertising agency, feeling restless and ready for a change. The couple met when Hicks landed en route from a modeling assignment, and now—sixteen years and four children later—they have several houses on the island, which are regularly filled with friends and family.

To reach Hibiscus Hill, you drive through an estate-like tropical garden at the top of a rise overlooking the town. Transformed from a 1950s Florida-style bungalow, it looks more like a Georgian-style tropical house and sits in a prominent central position on about three acres of palm tree–filled land. You first enter this comfortable family home through a long space divided into a dining and sitting room, which is anchored by a white marble fireplace—a relic left from a previous owner. However, Hicks and Flint Wood decided they liked its oddly appropriate French Caribbean style. The peaceful pastels of this room are accentuated by a large pink sofa, which sits opposite a sizable leather ottoman by Hicks's designer brother, Ashley Hicks.

The couple installed two walls of bookcases filled with curated family mementos as well as books. Some of the books have been re-covered with cream-colored paper and function as a backdrop for prints, small sculptural objects, and a large model of a yacht. The original cement-tiled floors have been replaced here with long, wide planks of fir, which help the house look substantially older than it really is.

A path leads from Hibiscus Hill down to the pink sands and extraordinary turquoise water of the famous Harbour Island beach.

ABOVE: *The side entrance to the house shows the added second-floor studios to the left. The outdoor dining loggia can be seen through the gates.* RIGHT: *A small Wendy house, built in the garden by Flint Wood for the children.*

ABOVE: *An added trellised porch by the front-door entrance provides shade for an outdoor living room near the pool.*
RIGHT, CLOCKWISE, FROM TOP LEFT: *Banger surveys the lunch table in the loggia. A white-painted mirror, console table, and door frames provide sharp contrast to the vivid red of the stairs leading up to the bedrooms. In the entry to the house you are greeted by India-designed fragrance sticks and a white tureen, which holds a handy collection of cricket balls. Red walls also act as a great backdrop for a collection of shells, kept tidy in a hanging bookcase.* FOLLOWING SPREAD: *Samson, a local potcake dog, sits uneasily on the Bahamian pink sofa in the sitting room. A studied collection of boxes, cases, and shells gives the coffee table an almost sculptural quality.*

ABOVE: *The sitting room walls are a custom blue-gray color,
which took three tries to get right due to the shifting tropical
light. The large leather ottoman was designed by Hicks's brother,
designer Ashley Hicks.* RIGHT: *The French fireplace came with
the house; it gives the room a hint of formality. Batman,
the cat, spends much of the day on a nearby slipcovered chair.*

LEFT: *Flint Wood designed the bookcases to hold books, hats, and family mementos.* RIGHT: *In front of books that had been re-covered in manila paper during a stretch of especially rainy weather sits a beautifully detailed model of a sailboat, which adds scale to the room.*

A crystal chandelier that came with the house adds sparkle to the dining table, although the family mainly eats out of doors near the kitchen under a sheltered porch. Most of the furniture in the house came from one epic trip to New Orleans, when the couple shipped twenty-two packing cases of furniture over to the island. Flint Wood has some reservations about this in retrospect, but happily most of the pieces fit the house or could be reworked or repainted to suit the various rooms. The family bedrooms are upstairs to take advantage of the cool breezes at night. The master bedroom is centered by a tall four-poster bed, which looks out across the garden, and taking up the original carpet revealed lively Cuban cement tiles from the 1950s, giving a touch of extra color to the room.

Removing the roof from a nearby kitchen structure and adding two upper rooms gave the couple twin studies, both decorated in radically different styles. Hicks obviously prefers a geometrical precision, no doubt inherited from her father, while Flint Wood's is a rich jumble of family mementos, tennis racquets, plans for design and architectural projects, and a very personal collection of paintings, many with an island theme. A short, sandy path from the house leads to a simple wooden gate, where the pink sands and iridescent blue water of the Bahamas lie just a few steps below.

ABOVE: *The couple added a wide-planked floor to the main areas of the house. The dining room is used during wet weather.* RIGHT: *The chandelier came with the house, while the dining table was found in New Orleans. The metal pineapple, a symbol of hospitality, is a recent addition.* FOLLOWING SPREAD: *Flint Wood's studio is a jumble of paintings, plans, and family projects. His long, antique Chinese desk is flanked at both ends of the room by built-in bookcases, which hold his library of primarily tropical-themed books. A folk art painting from Haiti rests on an easel to the left.*

LEFT: *A close-up of Flint Wood's bookcase featuring an antique box for watercolors and various small finds, including an ornamental coconut and a wooden obelisk.* ABOVE: *Here are several ways the household displays its shell collections.*

ABOVE: *The couple discovered the Anglo-Indian-style master bed in a catalogue. Called the Mountbatten, the bed refers to India's grandfather, Lord Mountbatten. Above the bed hang several nineteenth-century wood-engraved plates from their collection, produced by W. T. Greene of London.* RIGHT: *A close-up of a campaign chest in the master bedroom showing family photos, a bottle from Hicks's fragrance line, and the last flower left in the garden after Hurricane Irene had struck several days earlier.* FOLLOWING SPREAD: *The boys' bedroom, designed for the couple's two younger sons, Amory and Conrad, features a large British flag on the wall, found on Portobello Road in London, and twin beds shipped from New Orleans.*

Making Waves

SIMON DOONAN AND JONATHAN ADLER'S PALM BEACH APARTMENT

THOSE WHO ARE FAMILIAR WITH JONATHAN ADLER'S HIP, IRREVERENT STYLE AND HIS DECORATING BOOKS (*My Prescription for Anti-Depressive Living* and the follow-up Happy Chic series, including *Happy Chic Accessorizing* and *Happy Chic Colors*) will recognize the Palm Beach apartment he shares with his British partner, Simon Doonan, and their much-photographed dog, Liberace. Both are deeply involved with design. For many years Doonan has decorated the legendary windows of Barney's New York, while Adler owns fourteen eponymous stores that focus on home furnishings as well as his own pottery line.

Proving that you don't need a beach house to live by the sea, Adler and Doonan have decorated their vacation apartment in a cool, clear style that reflects their design heroes—an eclectic group that includes furniture designer Verner Panton and socialite designer Lilly Pulitzer, as well as famously stylish Babe Paley. They painted the walls white everywhere except the guest bedroom, which is painted a rich, dark brown, and added furniture and accessories in bright colors as accents. As a counterbalance, however, tabletops throughout the apartment are piled high with clusters of Adler's large white ceramic vases.

Entered through a double pair of front doors into the dining room, the main open living space is veiled by a vintage white metal screen made from outdoor gates, with matching Philippe Starck mirrors hanging on both sides. This also adds a sense of enclosure when sitting down to meals, where the centerpiece is an Adler-designed ceramic white shark—a nod to the nearby beach.

At one end of the main room, they have installed a table for table tennis, a reference to Doonan's past life in England. Invented in the nineteenth century by the upper classes, this energetic indoor game was first called "wiff-waff." Here, it is a decidedly modern affair, with Adler wallpaper decorating a very untraditional table, overlooked by a lively collection of "found" art.

Adler has broken up the space with a tête-à-tête sofa, which faces both sides of the long room. At the other end, he created a seating arrangement upholstered in a cheerful orange and a custom Adler-designed wall of ceramic teardrops. Scattered around the sofas is a collection of Adler's needlework cushions inspired by icons from the 1970s, like Liza Minnelli and Halston. However, Adler is careful to anchor his modernist designs with natural fibers and textiles; in this corner of the room he has used a large-scale jute rug, as well as a sisal carpet in the guest bedroom.

An Adler-designed ceramic greets
the day in the guest bedroom window
with a view out to the Atlantic.

ABOVE: *A view of the main living space. Glazed ceramic teardrops by Adler add to the beach feel of this predominantly all-white apartment.* RIGHT: *The Reef was designed in 1974 by Lawrence Group Architects; it has a central courtyard swimming pool.* FOLLOWING SPREAD: *The living room has been decorated in a combination of white and orange with sky-blue accents. Adler designed much of the furniture and pottery. However, the majestic white fiberglass Foo Dog on the balcony is one of a pair discovered at a Chinese restaurant.*

You can see the beach from the two bedrooms through the elegant 1960s-style wings of the apartment building by Lawrence Group Architects in 1974 (influenced by the work of Eero Saarinen), which was designed to give most units an ocean view. Outside, long balconies furnished with Philippe Starck white plastic outdoor furniture stretch along both sides of the building. The master bedroom is centered by a dramatic Paul Evans mirror bed, covered in a brightly colored suzani. Windows on two sides, framed by apple-green linen curtains, and the shimmer of the white walls make this an incredibly bright space. Leading from this room is a glamorous movie-star white marble bathroom.

Anyone who is lucky enough to stay with Adler and Doonan will enjoy the almost uninterrupted panorama of the sea—the guest bedroom has the best view of the whole apartment. The rich brown walls and bed piled high with cushions give the room an atmosphere of comfort and luxury. Here, as throughout the apartment, Adler has used orange as a color accent, which works well in almost any decorating scheme. The couple was helped enormously by proximity to the vintage shops in nearby West Palm Beach, and it did not take them long to discover a treasure trove from the 1960s and '70s, when Florida was a mecca for retirees.

Adler and Doonan enjoy the old-school glamour of Palm Beach, and their apartment is low maintenance enough for the busy couple to make stress-free visits whenever they need a break from the New York winter. Here, they can relax and indulge in their fashionable fantasies of matching caftans and "mocktails."

The dining room is separated from the main living space by a vintage screen crafted from outdoor gates. A pair of Philippe Starck mirrors hangs on both sides of the room divider. The painting is by Clement, from 1962. A wood and Plexiglas cabinet holds a collection of Adler-designed white vases.

ABOVE: *In the entry, a cheerful china dog holds hats for the beach.* RIGHT: *The Ping-Pong table is inventively covered in Adler wallpaper. On the right is a painting by the Italian artist Jean Calogero.*

ABOVE: *The mirrored master bed, by Paul Evans, is covered by a brightly colored suzani. Hanging on the wall is a giant carved silver dollar found in a Palm Beach thrift store.* RIGHT: *A close-up of a corner of the bedroom showing a careful composition of an Adler-designed pillow, vase, and side table mixed with local finds.* FOLLOWING SPREAD: *The guest bedroom features many of Adler's designs, from the wall plaques and the lamp right down to the pillows and sheets. He is known for his witty throw pillows.*

A Family House by the Sea

CLORA KELLY AND HELGE SKIBELI ON SHELTER ISLAND

SHELTER ISLAND IS A WELL-KEPT SECRET COMPARED TO THE GLITZY NEW YORK RESORT TOWNS of the Hamptons, which are famous for the celebrities who flock there every summer. Close to the Hamptons and reached by ferry, the small island consists of just over eleven and a half square miles, mostly of protected wetlands as well as the small, charming village of Dering Harbor. Houses here range from eighteenth-century Colonials to modern A-frames. The weekend beach house that Clora Kelly and her husband, Helge Skibeli, discovered was built in the 1880s and enlarged in the late 1920s. When they visited the property about five years ago, Kelly wasn't sure about the house at first, as it was dark and gloomy and needed major structural repairs. Skibeli saw more promise because the large house has uninterrupted water frontage. So they gutted it and rebuilt the interior. The biggest transformation occurred upstairs, where two floors of poky bedrooms were reworked to accommodate the couple's three children and lots of summer houseguests from Ireland and Norway. "I come from Ireland and lived near beautiful Georgian houses and wanted to keep as much of its character as possible," explains Kelly. During the eighteen-month renovation, she reused the original doors and flooring, added moldings and ceiling rosettes, and found an antique fireplace for a small room off the elegant living room. When Kelly redesigned the bathrooms, she kept to a timeless classic style, using plenty of white tile and old-fashioned claw-foot tubs, which meant that they fitted seamlessly into the nineteenth-century house.

As she had restored the traditional bones to the house, Kelly confidently dressed up the rest of the rooms with a mix of contemporary and antique furniture as well as bold modern art by American artists Andy Warhol, Kiki Smith, and Alex Katz. A striking piece, a brightly colored striped artwork—a collaboration between Kelly and her eleven-year-old daughter, Isa—dominates the master bedroom.

The award-winning New York neoclassicist architect Alfred Easton Poor had renovated the house nearly ninety years ago, adding impressive-looking columns to the front of the house and two spacious porches, one of which Kelly enclosed to create a dining room. She enjoyed rolling up her sleeves and working on the back wall herself, creating a bold backdrop of brown-and-white stripes for a cleverly balanced combination of old and new furniture. This space opens out from the big, central family kitchen, which is itself one of the most striking rooms of the house. Its high ceilings, white walls and floor, and stainless steel appliances cleverly bridge old and new. In this glamorous space, there are surprises: "The kitchen cabinets are from IKEA!" exclaims Kelly. A big marble-topped table anchors the space, surrounded by classic French bar stools designed by Xavier Pauchard in 1934.

Kelly's use of white throughout the house serves as a unifying backdrop, evident right from the entry, where an eclectic mix of furniture sits together, ranging from a nineteenth-century ornate table and an Art Deco chair to modern furniture and a floor lamp from IKEA. Somehow the combination of shapes and materials looks absolutely right. This room steps down into a long living room that runs along most of the front side of the house,

Kelly decorated the porch near the pool as an outdoor living room, with comfortable sofas and a pair of rattan floor cushions. FOLLOWING SPREAD: *The exterior of the late nineteenth-century house and its neoclassical façade renovated by Alfred Easton Poor nearly ninety years ago, as seen from the sea.*

Stairs lead from the entry to the upstairs bedrooms. An abstract painting by Ray Prohaska dominates the eclectic mix of furniture. FOLLOWING SPREAD: The main living spaces stretch the entire length of the house and all have views of the ocean. The white walls and floor act as a backdrop to the lively mix of furnishings in the sitting room. The 1940s silver and Lucite lamp was found locally on Shelter Island.

ABOVE: *The sitting room leads to this alcove, where a chrome and leather rocking chair combines with a Chesterfield sofa to create a comfortable corner in front of the fireplace.* RIGHT: *Kelly created a dramatic dining room from a porch at the other end of the house by painting the walls with broad, rich brown-and-white stripes. The nineteenth-century table and sideboard unexpectedly add to the modern vibe of the room.*

overlooking lawns that slope down to the water. Here, Moroccan rugs unify a collection of mainly modern furniture, including a spectacular white lacquer coffee table that had been found locally at one of Kelly's favorite stores. "Marika's is a wonderful antiques shop on Shelter Island," explains Kelly. A sprinkling of Asian furniture and objects adds to the eclecticism of this space, a reference to the years the couple spent in Singapore, which they used as a base to explore Southeast Asia. Tucked into a corner is a smaller space, where the couple likes to serve drinks in front of a fireplace Kelly found on the Internet. A striking element here is an unexpected chrome and leather rocking chair, also from Marika's, that sits happily alongside nineteenth-century-style upholstered furniture.

The swimming pool is reached through the remaining Poor-designed porch. Cooled by the sea breeze,

ABOVE: *The master bedroom carpets were inspired by English decorator David Hicks. An ethnic textile covers the bed; long silk curtains puddle on the floor.* RIGHT: *Together, Kelly and her daughter painted the striped canvas that hangs on the wall of the large master bedroom. Pucci silk cushions provide extra seating on the floor.* FOLLOWING SPREAD: *With its easy-to-clean white and stainless steel surfaces, the kitchen is the heart of this family's house by the sea. The cabinets are from IKEA, and the marble-topped table in the center is surrounded by 1930s Tolix stools.*

this is a popular place to hang out in the summer. Kelly has furnished it like a living room—with a sofa and movable rattan cushions. Upstairs, the large master bedroom happily accommodates the whole family, with a seating group at one end and an arresting pair of floor cushions upholstered in Pucci silk. Kelly designed the matching set of carpets commissioned while on a trip to India, which were inspired by English decorator David Hicks. Generous silk curtains frame the room's large windows, and a suzani textile is draped across the bed. In a nearby guest room, an impressive collection of tribal masks hangs on a wall by the bed. "I bought them at Marika's; I can't take credit, as I bought the whole display," says Kelly with a laugh.

She put the house together quickly. Kelly kept her furniture finds in the basement of their Manhattan town house and in a rented storage unit on Shelter Island. It took only a week to decorate—"I was pregnant with my son Otto at the time, and I just wanted to get it finished!" Kelly explains. Perhaps this is the answer to the house's fresh, original style. It has also impressed the family's many visitors. Shelter Island neighbor, decorator Tom Fallon, calls it "possibly the most original family home I have ever seen—a sophisticated blend of disparate shapes, styles, colors, scale, and textures. Her eye is bold, fearless, and perfect."

PART II: DESIGNS FOR BEACH LIVING

Outdoor Living

AUTHOR HENRY JAMES WROTE, "Summer afternoon . . . the two most beautiful words in the English language." It only gets better when you are by the beach. The whole point of living by the sea is to be able to entertain friends and family outdoors. Whether a picnic on the sand, a barbecue in the garden, or dinner on a terrace softly lit by paper lanterns or candelabra, this can easily become an unforgettable experience without too much effort.

One of the prettiest long tables I have ever seen by the beach was a line of doors resting on sawhorses, covered by identical blue bedspreads, with a row of freshly picked blue hydrangeas in vases down the middle. No one would have noticed that the chairs didn't match or that the plates were not in the same pattern, as this combination with the blue of the nearby ocean was dazzling.

Today there are plenty of wonderful and colorful choices of dinnerware, linens, flatware, and glasses available at very low prices in such stores as Cost Plus World Market, Pier 1 Imports, and Target. With easy online shopping, you can sit at home and plan your summer outdoor table settings in occasional spare moments. Keep to the same palette, and add another color as a lively accent. For example, combinations of blue and white are always right at the beach, but how about using red glasses? When buying tablecloths, consider that stripes and patterns seem to stay clean longer. There is nothing fresher than a lime green–striped tablecloth set with green and white leaf-patterned china and purple glasses. Have them shipped to the beach house so you can easily entertain in style.

Long summer evenings eventually turn to dusk, when outdoor lighting and bug repellent become important. Citronella candles are available as votives or in reusable pails that can be placed on the floor. Be creative with paper lanterns. You can get them in the same colors as your tablecloths; some are even battery operated, which means less complicated wiring chores. Another choice is solar-powered garden lights, which come on automatically as it gets dark.

In summer, you have more room outside to entertain. In sheltered areas there is no reason why you can't set up an outdoor living room, bringing some of the indoor furniture outside. Otherwise, there are all sorts of weatherproofed outdoor chairs and tables that can withstand the rain and ocean damp. Chairs made in PVC rattan look like the real thing, and acrylic-covered polyester seat cushions can be left outside during the season. Order them in colors that match your table settings. Adding stone tables and stucco benches will provide you with permanent outdoor furniture where you can sit year-round and enjoy the sea breezes.

PRECEDING SPREAD: *The ocean view from antiquarian Richard Shapiro's Malibu villa.* RIGHT: *A mint julep is a welcoming beach cocktail for hot weather entertaining.*

ABOVE: *A comfortably furnished porch with painted wicker at the Trident Hotel in Jamaica.* RIGHT: *A terrace under a shady tree is a great place to have lunch by the beach. All-weather furniture makes upkeep easier.* FOLLOWING SPREAD: *Outdoor space to entertain is important. Here, a spacious terrace designed for the Brignone family in Careyes, Mexico, has a breathtaking view of the ocean.*

LEFT: *Designer Muriel Brandolini put together a cheerful and informal lunch table overlooking the sea at her Hampton Bays beach house.* RIGHT: *Color is an important element of beach entertaining. Here, Martyn Lawrence Bullard designed a blue and white table with a view of the Mexican Pacific coast.*

ABOVE: *Landscapist Eric Nagelman designed this outdoor seating group for a home on the beach in Carpinteria, California.* RIGHT: *A canopied daybed by Carrido-Young Design in Newport, California, is an ideal place to spend time by a beachside swimming pool. Chinese ceramic stools serve as low-maintenance side tables.*

ABOVE: *India Hicks sets out watermelon on an outdoor table at her home in the Bahamas, Hibiscus Hill.* RIGHT: *Eric Nagelman created this display of watermelon on a terrace he designed in Carpinteria, California.*

ABOVE: *Architect Duccio Ermenegildo designed an outdoor dining room, including the table and chairs, for his house in Careyes, Mexico.* RIGHT: *Ermenegildo created an outdoor living room with built-in bench sofas for a beach house in the Dominican Republic.*

Collecting

ALMOST EVERYONE WHO SPENDS A SUMMER BY THE BEACH BRINGS HOME interesting finds—weathered glass, washed-up coral and seashells, or even bleached and curiously shaped tree branches and driftwood. Beachcombing is an irresistible part of living by the sea, and visiting local antiques shops and markets can be part of the fun too. Eventually a collection builds up; then you can start to display it somewhere where it can be enjoyed.

Bear in mind that objects are more effective in a group. You can mix and match them together to create a picture or tableau. Placement is important—sometimes a clear space between each object allows it to "breathe." Otherwise they can be grouped by color and texture for a more dramatic effect. Open shelves are great for displays, as well as mantelpieces and the tops of cupboards, side tables, and armoires. Windowsills are a good place for collections, especially colored glass, which becomes luminously backlit by the sun. Glassware of any kind always looks better en masse—on butler's trays, tabletops, and in every room in the house where light streams in.

Paintings, especially of water, boats, and other nautical themes, personalize a beach house. As the climate is harsh on original works, inexpensive vintage art pieces make the most sense at the beach; they can be found in flea markets and antiques stores. These look attractive when hung in groups or singled out above a sofa or bed, especially if a painting is large or dramatic.

There are many colors and patterns of china to collect. It is best to keep your collection simple—solid colors and off-whites or sea-related patterns in blue and white. Green majolica looks great on a table set for meals by the sea. Of course, there is nothing to stop you from collecting orange like Jonathan Adler, who is not afraid to use bold color at the beach. However, you will notice that his white walls work as a backdrop. When mixed with old pieces, new pottery and glass should be simple in form; vintage china tends to dominate visually because of its pattern and patina. Hutches or wall cabinets are an ideal place to display and store china, and they look good in every room. These are perfect places to showcase your collections, which can be mixed with found objects like shells, sea glass, and coral. These objects and other finds from the beach like skulls, branches, and driftwood add drama to an interior, especially when they are large in scale.

Shells can be used in many ways. Hot-glued to picture frames or small boxes, displayed on the coffee table, or on shelves with books, they are the common thread that runs through every beach collection. Large or small, they always add visual interest and texture and a beach-house feeling to any room.

Don't forget everyday objects like straw hats or beach shoes, which can be attractively clustered in large baskets—even piles of beach towels can be decorative. As your beach place is often a second house, this is your chance to be creative and take risks that you wouldn't think of in your year-round home. Collections can be big and bold with bright, colorful backgrounds. Have fun—after all, when summer is over they can all be taken down for a fresh start next year.

Even the top of an armoire can be pressed into service as a place to display an impressive amount of coral.

Decorator Steven Gambrel lined up a collection of glass urns on his honey-colored stripped-wood period fireplace in his Sag Harbor home.

ABOVE: *Sri Lankan oil lamps become more interesting when grouped together in a row.* RIGHT: *Steven Gambrel displays glass against a window to emphasize its color.* PAGE 220: *The open shelves of a bookcase near a dining table holds a range of Steven Gambrel's cream and white pottery, enlivened by the clear reflective glass of several decanters.* PAGE 221: *On Harbour Island, the de Givenchy family displays a variety of collections in a glass-fronted bookcase.*

ABOVE: *Here are different ways to style shell collections in ornamental groupings.* RIGHT: *Designer Laura Clayton Baker showcases her sea glass collection in wooden goblets and bowls.*

Swimming Pools

SWIMMING POOLS HAVE BEEN PART OF LIFE BY THE SEA IN AMERICA since the Olympic Games of 1896, when swimming races were among the original events. The popularity of swimming pools spread, and today they not only add to the resort atmosphere of a beach house but are invaluable when the ocean is too rough or far away or below a steep cliff. Once a symbol of luxury and leisure, pools have become more affordable than ever with new products and construction techniques. In many cases, a pool offers a backdrop to entertaining—with an outdoor barbecue conveniently near the kitchen—and a focal point for an afternoon with close friends.

The first step to planning a pool is to work out the appropriate design style that suits your house and grounds. It should become part of the architecture of the property, enclosed by walls or columns that form part of a beach house or villa and shelter it from winds and provide extra privacy. The free-form swimming pool is not as fashionable today as a more rectangular style, which can double as an ornamental pond and architectural feature when not in use. An elegant terrace, perhaps with an inset pattern or design, can combine with the pool's sheet of water to look like an art installation, or you can add large-scale plant pots at each corner to give a more formal look. Hot tubs are usually incorporated into swimming pools and often add to their size and scale.

Location is another big decision. Depending on your ocean view, there are many different styles and creative opportunities in designing a swimming pool. One of the most dramatic is the infinity pool, in which an open edge of the pool appears to meet seamlessly with the sea. This design, which evolved at resort hotels in Bali in the 1980s, gives a real elegance to the garden, although it needs a slight rise in topography for the full effect. Whether it is a large or small pool, this also works when your sea view is far away—it naturally draws attention to the horizon.

Some people are lucky to own a place directly on the sand, which may be a problem on a busy city beach. One of the best solutions I have ever seen is a high wall that can be opened like a sliding door to reveal the sand during less trafficked times of the day. This gives the glorious illusion that you own the beach, which lasts just as long as the next group of Rollerbladers breezes past.

Landscaping around the pool is important, especially as safety regulations require fencing and gates, which can be incorporated into well-designed features like hedges, stone walls, or surrounding enclosures. Today, more than ever, you need the advice of a skilled landscape designer, who can also incorporate cooking and dining areas with the decking around the pool to help you make the most of outdoor entertaining. Often there is space to build a structure, such as a gazebo, a cabana, or just an overhead trellis, which you should plan to relate stylistically to your house. Keep the pool furniture minimal, using the same scale and color, so that it doesn't overwhelm the garden.

Finally, after what seems like a long construction process, a pool will transform your beach house into a relaxing resort by the sea, where you can happily host a multitude of lunches, barbecues, and dinner parties under the stars.

RIGHT: *The swimming pool at a beach house designed by architect John Lautner in Malibu is cleverly folded into the wings of the building.* FOLLOWING SPREAD: *Giancarlo Brignone's swimming pool in Careyes, Mexico, is an art installation that includes the ocean as part of the design.*

ABOVE: *An infinity-edge pool adds drama to a view of the Malibu coast.* RIGHT: *Mark Cutler decorated this modern beach house in Santa Monica, California. The gates at the end of the pool close to provide privacy from the public beach when necessary.*

ABOVE: *The author contemplates the sea in a small infinity pool at the Four Seasons Hotel in Bali. Landscaped by Made Wijaya, each villa's pool has a view of the ocean.* RIGHT: *Architect Duccio Ermenegildo designed this elegant swimming pool in the Dominican Republic.*

Artist MariCarmen Hernandez built a lap pool on the beach of her house in Troncones, Mexico. The rope swing makes a good diving board.

ABOVE: *The pondlike shape of this swimming pool suits the nineteenth-century-style housing at Strawberry Hill in Jamaica.*
RIGHT: *Steven Gambrel added a small lap pool, which doubles as an ornamental pond at the back of his Sag Harbor house.*

CLOCKWISE, FROM TOP LEFT: *An infinity pool in Careyes, Mexico, connects visually with a distant ocean view. A similar pool in Phuket, Thailand, with a straighter edge. This Santa Monica hot tub by Barry Beer is separated from the pool by a sturdy glass enclosure. Designer Brad Dunning worked on this Malibu house, where the pool has a built-in hot tub.* RIGHT: *Broad steps lead down to fashion designer Tommy Hilfiger's swimming pool built directly on the sand in Mustique.*

Designer Directory

The following architects, interior designers, designers, and antiques dealers have houses or design projects featured in this book, and several have their own furnishing lines, shops, and books.

Jonathan Adler
800-963-0891
www.jonathanadler.com

Spencer Croul
www.surfingheritage.org

John Derian Company
6 East Second Street
New York, New York 10003
212-677-3917
www.johnderian.com

Peter Dunham Design
909 North Orlando Avenue
Los Angeles, California 90069
323-848-9900
www.peterdunham.com
and
Hollywood at Home
724 and 750 North La Cienega
Boulevard
Los Angeles, California 90069
310-273-6200
www.hollywoodathome.com

English Country Antiques
26 Snake Hollow Road
Bridgehampton, New York
11932
631-537-0606
www.ecantiques.com

Duccio Ermenegildo Architect
917-378-6770
derenegildo@gmail.com

Tom Fallon Design
4 Washington Street
Shelter Island Heights
Shelter Island, New York 11965
917-601-3857
www.tomfallondesign.com

India Hicks
www.indiahicks.com
www.sugarmillbyindiahicks.com
www.hibiscushillharbourisland.com

Zoë Hoare
www.chezzoe.net

Martyn Lawrence Bullard
Design
8550 Melrose Avenue
Los Angeles, California 90069
323-655-5080
www.martynlawrencebullard.com

Juan Montoya Design
330 East 59th Street
New York, New York 10022
212-421-2400
www.juanmontoyadesign.com

Matthew Rolston
www.matthewrolston.com

Ted Russell Interior Design
1875 Carla Ridge
Beverly Hills, California 90210
310-275-1609

Tom Scheerer
215 Park Avenue South, #1701
New York, New York 10003
212-529-0744
www.tomscheerer.com

Richard Shapiro Antiques
and Works of Art
Studiolo
8905 Melrose Avenue
Los Angeles, California 90069
310-275-6700
www.studiolo.com

Made Wijaya
ptwijaya.com
madewijaya2@gmail.com

RIGHT: *A tall Mexican fountain in a Punta Mita courtyard.*

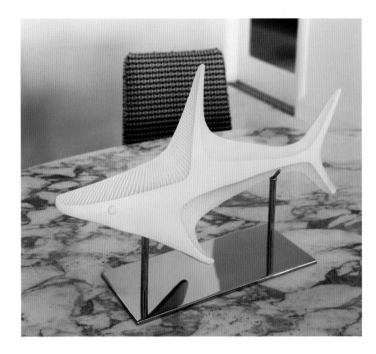

A ceramic shark, created by Jonathan Adler, sits on his Palm Beach dining table.

First published in the United States of America in 2012
by Rizzoli International Publications, Inc.
300 Park Avenue South
New York, New York 10010
www.rizzoliusa.com

Photography copyright © 2012 Tim Street-Porter

2012 2013 2014 2015/ 10 9 8 7 6 5 4 3 2 1

Printed in China

ISBN 13: 978-0-8478-3838-7

Library of Congress Control Number: 2011942137

Project Editor: Sandra Gilbert
Art Direction: Doug Turshen with Steve Turner